When Can a Child Believe?

Eugene Chamberlain

BROADMAN PRESS
Nashville, Tennessee

4262-08
ISBN: 0-8054-6208-2

Dewey Decimal Classification: 234
Printed in the United States of America

"When can a child believe?" is the most serious question parents ever face. This book is lovingly dedicated to the three people who live at my house and who have helped me learn through experience most of what I know about how to answer the question:

> Dorothy, my wife
> Barry, my son
> Marigene, my daughter

Contents

Foreword   7

1. Why Talk About It?   9

2. Whose Child Is He?   19

3. Is He Lost?   30

4. Would You Believe What He Did?   38

5. What Are the Signs?   49

6. How Do You Talk Religion to a Child?   56

7. Where Are the Roots?   66

8. Who Can Help?   74

When, Indeed?   80

Foreword

Who would deny that parents and children's workers as well are confused about children and the matter of conversion? We are afraid to push, and we are afraid not to push. Our confusion is the result of many forces which shape us and our churches.

So? So I propose to help at least one segment of the Christian community to handle its confusion with a greater degree of calm and insight. That segment is parents who are lay people. The things I say should also help workers with children, those who teach children in church organizations and who seek to serve children in other ways. The book should also prove helpful to others outside traditional church channels who are concerned with winning children to Christ. In fact, anyone—theologian, educator, or what-have-you—who is genuinely interested in children is invited to read along.

The book is more like a chat between two parents than like a formal treatise on the subject of conversion. No one need expect deep theological discourses. Don't look for lofty treatment of obscure doctrinal points. Don't anticipate super psychology.

Do be ready for as much give-and-take as the structure of the book permits. Here and there you will find suggestions for things to do. Take these suggestions seriously, and you will discover yourself talking back to me.

When the conversation is over, I hope you will be thinking prayerfully about one of the most important matters which we as churches and individuals face today. I hope you will have found, here or within yourself, help for guiding the spiritual development of children, your own or those belonging to others.

1
Why Talk About It?

"Say, there's something Rose and I have been wanting to talk over with you." The young man who had stopped me in a church hallway continued, "Jimbo has been talking more and more about becoming a Christian. Well, actually he is talking about being baptized. You've had Jimbo in Sunday School, and we'd appreciate your telling us what you think. We don't want to do the wrong thing."

Does that daddy sound like most any typical parent of an eight-year-old who is raising questions about conversion? Actually this man was a church staff member with a strong background in theology and psychology. His wife, a schoolteacher, had formerly been a church staff member with responsibility for children's work. Yet they were just as troubled as any other set of parents you might name.

Their experience underscores a basic problem churches confront today. Parents and children's workers, too, are confused about how to deal with a child who expresses a growing and genuine concern about his spiritual condition.

Evidences of Confusion

This confusion is evidenced in many ways. For instance, consider the evasive language many parents and workers use when talking about conversion.

Ask a number of parents if all of their children are Christians. Too often you get this response: "My children have all been baptized." If the parent comes from a church which equates baptism with conversion, this answer is not too surprising. But if the parent comes from an evangelical communion, you wonder what keeps him from simply saying yes.

Or try asking if all of the children have accepted Christ as Savior. One of the frequent answers is, "They are all church members." If the parent comes from a faith which makes church membership and a profession of faith one and the same, you aren't too surprised. But the parent who comes from a church which makes sharp distinction between the two acts should answer you yes or no.

Talk to a parent about the need of his child for Christ. "He isn't a bad boy," he will say. Another parent will say of his child, "Oh, he has always loved Jesus." Neither comment, of course, has much to do with the matter.

Parents are, it seems, divided into two camps. One is afraid of holding back a child in the matter of his personal profession of faith in Christ. The other is just as alarmed at the thought of pushing a child. Frequently one parent is torn by both fears. And workers find themselves in the same boat in regard to their own children as well as in regard to the children they teach.

Sources of Confusion

Parents take in stride most major happenings in the lives of their children. Why do they suffer so much confusion about conversion?

One of the most significant factors contributing to this confusion is a general lack of understanding of conversion. All of us know that a person's experience with God is his, and his alone. For this reason, and perhaps for others, we are reluctant to pass judgment upon what is going on in the heart of any person, even one so well known to us as our own child. We stand aside, nervously wondering if what the child says means what it might mean.

We aren't quite sure just what is involved in a profession of faith anyway. Even if we ourselves are Christians, we are afraid that the child's understanding is too weak. Or we are uncertain that his theology is adequate. Perhaps as we grow in grace through the years, we lose sight of what was involved in our own conversion. Or our memories become clouded by more recent spiritual experiences. Or even remembering clearly, we are afraid that the distinctively personal elements in our children's experiences make those experiences something less than valid.

Take a moment right now. Try to recall your own conversion. How old were you? Where were you? What experiences preceded the actual making of your profession? How did you feel about the whole experience?

A parent who is not a Christian faces a different situation. He may never have faced squarely his personal spiritual need. Or he may long since have rejected Christ's claims upon him. He cannot easily compare his child's situation to his own and encourage the child to respond positively to God's love as expressed in Jesus Christ.

Later in this book, we'll talk together about what conversion is. That discussion should help you, whether a Christian or not, to think through your own spiritual experience more clearly. Our talk may also help you understand the ways in which your experience continues to influence you in your dealing with children. Perhaps that discussion will prompt you to more profound and detailed study on your own.

Tied to inadequate understanding of conversion is inadequate understanding of the meaning of church membership. Yet until a child is fully enrolled as a church member, many parents and workers are uneasy. A naggy little suspicion says the Lord may not have the child's name if we haven't written it on our church roll.

Another major factor in parental (and worker) confusion is the advice they receive. When a parent expresses doubt about how to proceed with his child, he gets conflicting responses.

He hears: "You certainly don't want to hold a child back. You know my cousin, John Johnson. And you know what a rounder he is. Would you believe that he once wanted to join the church? His mother wouldn't hear to it. And he quit going at all."

Or he hears: "Well, you certainly do want to be sure that he understands what he is doing. You know my cousin, John Johnson. And you know what a rounder he is. His mother was determined that all of her children would join the church as early as possible. She pushed John and his religious life never has amounted to anything."

Another cause of confusion is evangelists, pastors, and workers who treat young children as legitimate targets for evangelism. In all churches and in other settings, too, you encounter people who feel that regardless of a child's age or experience he should be confronted with the claims of the gospel. The point will become clear as you continue reading.

While attending a small party, I overheard the hostess talking to a friend of mine whose special interest was childhood education. "My daughter," said the hostess, "is so interested in helping children. Even though she is still in high school, she gathers the neighborhood children in our family room about once a week. They play games and sing songs. She tells them Bible stories. She always invites them to accept Jesus. And so many of these children have."

"Tell me more about her group," my friend prompted.

The woman continued: "Well, they come and go. It isn't always the same group. Sometimes they come and bring little friends with them."

"How old are most of the children?"

"Oh, they range from three up into elementary school."

Have you attended worship services which were climaxed by invitations for young children to profess faith in Christ? When I hear a pastor say, "There may be a young boy or girl here who should come and tell us that he loves Jesus," I wonder how young is young. Any child hearing the invitation would consider himself at least as old as a "young boy or girl."

Unfortunately, thoughtful workers and parents face problems more serious than poorly worded invitations. There are persons and organizations whose practices indicate their belief that any person capable of expressing any sort of affirmative response to Jesus' love is ready for the conversion experience. Often this affirmative response amounts to no more than the raising of a hand when asked a question such as, "Do you love Jesus?" We must not let the apparent sincerity of such people blind us to the catches in their basic theological assumptions.

A further cause of confusion about conversion and the young child is inept counseling by well-meaning persons. All of us have seen a young child respond to the pastor's invitation to make a profession of faith. In the hearing of the congregation, the pastor asked the child some questions about himself and his feelings toward Christ and the church. Each question was a good one—with one terrible exception: each answer was obviously either yes or no. Even a child who had just walked in off the street would know how the pastor expected him to answer the questions. Although the child's decision proved valid, a bad side effect had taken place. An entire congregation had been encouraged to think that making one's decision for Christ is just a matter of answering a few yes-or-no questions.

In the olden days, many Sunday School workers felt they had utterly failed if any child over the age of nine spent a year in their groups without making a profession of faith. With today's current trends to younger and younger conversions, one is not surprised if workers with younger children now feel the stigma of failing to convert their charges. The insidious thing about protesting against a worker's setting such a goal is that one appears to be opposed to winning children at all. Still the very fact that such goals are set creates a climate of confusion. If such goals are set by concerned persons, a parent naturally reasons that his child must be a legitimate object for conversion no matter how immature the child appears to be.

The presumption of such goal setting is breath-taking. How can Christians forget that in promising the Holy Spirit, Jesus told us that it is the Holy Spirit who convicts of sin? (See John 16:1-11.)

Another source of confusion is, strangely enough, the testimony of Christians who were converted at an early age. Some years ago I participated in a study group which explored this whole business of early conversion and of the factors involved in a child's ability to receive the gospel. Most of those in the group indicated that their conversion had taken place anywhere from their ninth year on. A few indicated that they had been converted much earlier.

As the conversation progressed, the group seemed to move toward a consensus that few, if any, children were likely to be fit objects for overt evangelism any earlier than about the ninth year. At this point, one of the women protested strongly. "But I was converted when I was six. I knew that I needed Christ. I accepted him then. I have never had any reason to doubt my conversion," she declared firmly.

The effect of such testimonies is varied. Some parents listen and find assurance that the profession their young child seems to be about to make can be genuine. Other parents hear and feel that they had better get busy with their own youngster. If one can be saved at so early an age, they reason, then any child of this age who has not made a profession of faith must be lost.

In addition, some forces at work in our culture tend to make us expect and work for conversion at a younger age than we once did. Look at the movement toward providing formal educational experiences for children we once thought too young for anything except "play." Look at the way parents introduce children to adult-type social activities at an earlier and earlier age. How old were you before you had a formal or wore a tux? How old are most children today when they are encouraged to dress like and act like adults at adultish parties? How late into life did you play sandlot baseball or scrub football? Did your parents concern themselves with cheering at neighborhood games? Yet how old is today's boy when he begins to participate in highly organized sports? What happens if you miss one of his games? When we treat children as miniature adults in other areas of life, it is natural for us to expect them to make professions of faith at a tender age.

Nor can anyone blame us for feeling that a child's constant exposure to information means earlier maturity. When an average adult can scarcely understand the technical language with which children handle the space age, he can scarcely help feeling that children are more mature today than he was at the same age. The nonchalance of today's children in handling mathematical equations lulls one into feeling that they are better equipped to handle life's difficult equations than their parents were at the same age.

But probably one of the greatest sources of confusion is simply the fact that too few adults and children are on good talking terms in the area of the inner life. Perhaps because helping a child explore his inner life is difficult, we simply don't try. We tend to dismiss with amusement a child's early struggles to express himself. Or we jump to the conclusion that the child is some sort of spiritual giant with perceptions not seen among men since the day of the great Old Testament prophets or Paul. Neither attitude is conducive to developing a solid base upon which a parent (or worker) and child can talk about what is taking place in the child's heart and mind.

I've said a lot about the tender age at which children are now making professions of faith, assuming that you were aware of this fact. For a moment, suppose we take a look at what statistics indicate about this picture among Southern Baptists. There is no reason to assume that the trends are greatly different in other groups.

Up into the 1950's, the norm for conversion was about nine to ten years. By 1966-67, the picture had changed drastically. For that year, churches in the denomination reported 1,146 baptisms among children under six years of age. An additional 34,026 baptisms were reported among children six through eight years of age.[1] Together the total number of baptisms of children below nine years of age constituted nearly 10 percent of all conversions reported for that year. As yet there seems to be no reversal in this trend.

The "Or Else"

If for one moment you doubt that the issue which we are discussing is important, think what we can expect if we do not work out better approaches. The results form an ominous "or else."

We will continue to have churches filled with unregenerate church members. Regardless of the age at which children face

---

[1] *Quarterly Review*, October-December, 1967, pp. 22-31.

this decision, they deserve sound guidance. If more children are to become Christians and church members at an earlier age, let them do so with better and better guidance from their parents and workers.

We will continue to deal with an increasing number of bewildered youth. Children who do not receive adequate help in dealing with spiritual matters become youth who cannot cope successfully with the problems of the inner life.

We will continue to produce impotent churches. Strong churches are not built upon adults who are unregenerate or upon youth who are bewildered.

We can expect spiritual dwarfs even among those who are genuinely converted. Hearts opened to God need nourishment. The climate for such development is not created by those whose own spiritual stature is stunted and twisted.

For You to Do

Why are you reading this book? Exactly what do you hope to gain? Can you state a reason clearly and simply? Taking time to do so now will make the book all the more meaningful to you.

One way to fix your purpose clearly in mind is to mark the paragraphs or sentences in this chapter which you feel clearly identify you and your concerns. Underscore those sentences, or place a mark of some sort in the margin opposite them. Then reread the marked sentences and paragraphs.

If you can state your purpose clearly, you are more than ready to keep reading.

A Parent's Prayer

I'm scared, God.
I'm not at all certain that I'm fit or able to guide this
   child you have entrusted to me.

I listen to the voices around me.
The voices confuse me.
The voices frighten me.
I cannot guide this child alone.
Dear Lord, may I offer him to you?
Not like Hannah giving Samuel,
I don't really know how to do that.
I mean, may I trust you to guide my efforts to guide him?
May I have faith that you will somehow offset the mistakes I am sure to make?
May I have confidence that you will do what is best for him?
If so, I can be content to do the best I can for him.

2
Whose Child Is He?

The discussion at coffee break went like a lot of coffee break discussions do. It centered on children.

"Sometimes on weekends I feel like a human taxi," groaned the father of two teen-agers still too young to drive.

"That's why it is more of a relief than a worry when they get a license," responded the woman across the table.

"I agree," chipped in another dad. "I know you're supposed to worry and worry about them when they begin to drive. But, man, the release not to have to be running here and running there every minute of the weekend!"

A fourth member of the group looked thoughtful and then said, "This taxi business is just a symptom of something that really troubles me about family life. The American pattern of living forces a family to rely too heavily upon itself. A mother and a father are expected to be all things in all things and to do all things for their kids."

"But you aren't serious," someone asked, "about this taxi business amounting to more than an inconvenience, are you?"

"I'm thinking how few families today have any larger family to help with day-to-day living, much less crises."

The human taxi spoke up: "If my dad lived nearby, he'd probably enjoy doing some of the routine running we do for the kids. And I can tell you we could sure have used some 'larger family' when Bev was so ill."

Your Child Is Ours

The feelings expressed at that coffee break are especially
interesting when one thinks about all the organizations which
seem ready to share parental responsibility. As a rule, each
organization assumes responsibility in a restricted area of the
child's life.

Take, for instance, your church. Depending upon several
factors, your church may offer an astounding variety of experiences for your child. Sunday School is most surely one. There
may also be additional church-related learning opportunities
on Sunday night and during the week. Your church may have
organizations for church training, music, and missions. Your
child may easily spend five to six hours each week in such
situations without counting service activities and parties.

The important factor, however, is not the amount of time
the child spends at the church. The significant thing is the
claims which the church makes, explicitly or implicitly, about
what it will do for the child—and for you, the parent. Where
does your church fix ultimate responsibility for the spiritual
welfare of the child? Do you sense that the church will take
care of things if you just get your child to the church? Or
would you say that your church throws responsibility for your
child's spiritual welfare back on you, the parent?

Who sees that your child grows intellectually? Not long ago
I listened to a math teacher explain his view of the parents'
role as related to his own. "I tell my students not to expect
mother and daddy to help them. If they need help, tell me.
We'll get the answers," he said. In spite of all the fun, fury,
and agony of raising money, directly or through taxes, a large
body of parents feels that the school has taken over any real
responsibility they might have had as developers of their chil-

dren's intellectual lives.

And who is willing to take on your child's physical development? On the surface, one might think that a lot of organizations are. Certainly the elementary schoolboy can play football, baseball, and basketball from one end of the calendar to the other under the direction of one group or another.

Even our children's cultural development seems to be the responsibility of groups outside the home. Of course, mamma and poppa must pay the bills for lessons and tickets.

They are all there, the child-developers—waiting for, demanding, grabbing for parental support. In exchange for the price of tickets, lessons, uniforms, bus fares, and being the "human taxi," you are assured that your child will have the best of all which life offers. One wonders whether the promises can possibly be kept.

Parental Responsibility in the Spiritual Life

In our discussion, of course, we are interested most of all in the spiritual aspect of life. We are concerned with other areas as they impinge upon spiritual growth. Our basic question, therefore, is: What is the parent's relationship to his child in the area of spiritual growth?

That question gets a lot of different answers. At one extreme is a hands-off attitude. You've heard: "My mother made me go to church, and there's one thing I'm not going to do. I'm not going to force religion down my child's throat. He can make up his own mind."

You can pick flaws immediately in this sort of reasoning. A child who is begged and wheedled to eat but who knows that his parent will make no effort to involve him in Sunday School and church usually decides that spiritual food is not very important. In this case, the adult who wanted his child to be free to make his own choice has already made it difficult for the child to make sound choices in the spiritual realm.

At the other extreme stands the parent who is determined to mold and shape the child, content with an outward appearance of piety and too frequently without much regard for the child's inner life. One parent talked with another about his child's struggle to understand the meaning of church membership. The boy was troubled about joining the church because he would be expected to vote on matters such as the church budget. He realized that he did not understand such matters well enough to make choices.

The second parent merely shrugged. "I just tell mine how to vote," was his comment.

Telling a child how to vote on a church budget may not be too important. Assuming that you can settle matters related to a child's inner struggle so simply is dangerous.

Most of us parents probably view our relationship to our children in the area of spiritual growth as lying somewhere between these two extremes. We are likely to view ourselves as leaders along a path which we have travelled. Without being so directive as the "tell-'em-how-to-vote" father, we may still tend to tell a child how things are and expect him to take our word for it. We may be inclined to think, because we have gained our viewpoint through experience, that our child will inevitably come to share that viewpoint.

You may prefer other words to describe this relationship. "Guide" is used with some frequency. Perhaps those who prefer "guide" see themselves as stepping in at crucial points to give direction, rather than pacing every step of the trail.

Some of us like the term "teacher." This term suggests that the parent opens up the child's insights and helps to equip him to make sound choices. As a rule, those who think of themselves as teachers still feel that they know which choices are right for the child.

One to Think About

I would like to offer a concept for you to consider. At our house we have found this concept valuable. If we had reared a thousand children using the concept, perhaps we could give you statistical *proof* of its worth. Deep down we suspect that proofs are hard to come by in the area we are discussing. So take the idea and think about it.

As a parent seeking to help my child grow spiritually, I see myself as a fellow adventurer on an exciting road. Though I have already travelled part of the road, my child and I are now travelling together. I have not reached the end of the road—and shall not within my lifetime on earth. I cannot take my child's steps for him, but I can assure him that the Christian life is a rich and rewarding experience. I can say: "Let's hike along together. I'll help you whenever I can. And I know you'll help me, too."

What Can My Church Do?

No matter what view a parent takes of his relationship to his child in the area of the child's spiritual growth, he still must decide how much of his responsibility he can afford to turn over to others and how much he must handle himself. You and I must listen to the pleas and promises of others, individuals and groups, and weigh carefully their ability to do what they say they can do. We must consider their basic religious concepts before we commit a child of ours to their keeping. We would not commit the spiritual nurture of a child to the proponents of some pagan religion just because these people asserted themselves to be spiritual men. Yet we are all too careless about trusting children to any group calling itself Christian. For instance, parents who claim to believe that baptism is only symbolic often hand over the religious training of their children to groups or persons who believe baptism saves. This sort of practice is almost sure to cause a child to be confused about basic religious teachings.

The important point to remember is that no parent can give away his responsibility. Even the choice of others to help him meet his responsibility must be carefully made. One could advance theological reasons for placing responsibility upon the parent. Maybe all that is needed is the half-humorous observation: "If the Lord had intended churches to rear children, he would have managed to get them born to churches, not to mothers and daddies."

Practical considerations also underscore this basic truth. Until we restructure our society so that parents play a less significant role in the life of a child, parents will continue to be the major force in shaping a child's life.

This truth does not, of course, rule out a parent's getting help from his church. Let's think a few minutes about what a parent may reasonably expect from his church.

Obviously, the parent can expect his church to provide basic Bible teaching. The child who goes regularly to Sunday School and to other functions of his church will surely acquire a basic understanding of Bible facts. Surely he will also acquire some insight into the meaning of the facts he acquires. However, a parent is an ostrich if he thinks that a couple of hours of instruction a week, even taken on a consistent basis, are going to provide his child *all* the spiritual knowledge and insight he will need to become a mature Christian. The church settings in which children are taught are inevitably artificial or, to say the least, somewhat removed from life itself. The religious teachings which the parent provides take place within the framework of real life itself.

Second, a parent can rightfully expect his church to provide support to him in guiding his child. Churches with genuine concern for children provide training groups and reading materials for parents. In such groups, a parent can talk out some of the frustrations he experiences in guiding his child. Through his church, he can explore the deeper meanings of parenthood, both within and without the Christian community.

In the third place, a parent can expect his church to provide a climate in which his child can explore Bible truth and discover the meaning of salvation and Christian discipleship. Much of this climate is created by the existence of the fellowship within which the child is accepted for what he presently is as well as for what he can, under God, become. A parent can expect fellow Christians who make up the fellowship to share personal experiences with him and with his child in such a way that both he and the child benefit. In times of distress, even when he or his child has made serious mistakes, a parent can expect his church to provide comfort and guidance. In times of great joy, he can expect his church to provide the sharing which enables a person to experience his own joy more deeply and to interpret the experience in the light of Christian teaching.

Does all of this sound like too much to expect from a group of people who are, after all, human? Even though these promises are fulfilled imperfectly, most church bodies do try to be just this to those who are part of their fellowship.

For You to Do

Review this section in the light of what you expect from your church. Take a moment to write here what you expect. Later you may wish to share your ideas with others in your church—your pastor, other leaders, other parents like yourself.

_____

_____

_____

_____

What About Other Religious Groups?

Of course, religious groups other than one's church are willing, even eager, to assume some of the responsibility which ultimately rests upon parents. To assume that all groups which profess religious ends are suited or equipped to meet the needs of one's child is dangerous. At the same time, it is foolish to assume that all religious groups outside one's own circle have devious reasons for wishing to play a role in the religious development of children. Just what guidelines should a parent use in determining to which groups he may entrust his child?

The most basic question is: What view does the group in question have of salvation? The answer to this question affects virtually everything a group does. The answer is reflected in songs as well as in sermons. The basic pattern of meetings or other activities is rooted in this basic viewpoint. If the viewpoint of the group differs radically from your own view, you can anticipate more difficulty than help if you permit the group to help your child handle a confrontation with Christ. Listening to varying voices is difficult enough for a child at best, much less when his parent tacitly or actively endorses conflicting views of this basic experience.

A second and, perhaps, equally important question is: What is the group's view of the church? This statement does not infer that no group with a weakly defined concept of the church can be genuinely Christian. But the church plays an important role in the life of every maturing Christian. The Bible plainly teaches that we are not to be Christians in some sort of vacuum. You do a disservice to your child when you encourage his participation in groups which downgrade or minimize the role of the church in the Christian life.

Linked to these questions is another: What follow-up does the group offer to those who profess Christ as an outgrowth of its activities? A group which strives only to get a child to say, "I take Jesus as my Savior," and then abandons him does not meet his deepest needs. A new Christian must be fed the milk of the Spirit before he can eat meat. He must eventually learn to handle meat if he is to become fully mature.

Another question to ask is: What techniques does the group employ to guide a child in making a profession? Some groups which report outstanding success with children use a great deal of symbolism. Black stands for sin. White stands for purity. Red stands for Christ's shed blood. Clean hands stand for a good life. Dirty hands stand for the unregenerate life. Young children simply cannot understand such symbolism.

Even in the later elementary school years many children have extreme difficulty with symbolism. They simply don't get the message. Without minimizing the role of the Holy Spirit in the life of the child, it seems safe enough to say that very few young children get the point of such presentations. Their apparent positive responses are not to the message so much as to the tone of the message or to the personality of the messenger.

Some groups which deal with children offer rewards to prompt decisions. No one gives candy for making a profession. Yet an adult who helps a child identify himself with the "good guys" when he says the right words is offering a reward. A negative reward is invoked when a child who fails to make the right statement becomes (or remains) a "bad guy." Even in our rejoicing over one child's decision, we may place another child under great pressure to imitate his friend to win acceptance for himself.

A final question a parent should ask himself about religious groups to which he is tempted to entrust his child may seem more simple than the others. Does the group mix children of all ages in making its approaches? This question is significant because of the rapid development of children. A three-year-old is not ready to deal with the spiritual concerns of a ten-year-old, much less cope with a vocabulary meant for a ten-year-old. To simplify approaches so that a three-year-old can understand what is going on forces one to feed the ten-year-old something considerably less than he needs.

Can you answer these basic questions about religious groups outside your church which bid for your child's interest and attention? Taking time to find the answers can make the difference between providing sound guidance for your child and introducing him into a period of floundering. The answers may help you avoid not only upsetting him but serious spiritual problems for yourself and for others in your household as well.

Something Else for You to Do

Do your best to give honest answers to the questions in this section. Then use your answers to reevaluate your responsibility in guiding your child and in measuring the way in which you are meeting that responsibility.

• To what extent do I feel responsible for my child's spiritual development?

• What word or term would I use to describe my relationship to my child in the area of his spiritual development?

• How regularly do I help my child take advantage of the opportunities our church offers for his spiritual development?

• How actively do I seek to understand the work of the Sunday School and other church organizations to which my child belongs?

• In what ways do I expect my church to help me in guiding my child's spiritual development?

• How well do I follow up on church experiences which my child has?

• Do I carefully investigate other religious groups to which my child is invited?

• What effort do I make to help my child interpret and

understand the experiences which he has in connection with religious groups outside our church?

A Parent's Prayer

I call him "my child."
Is he really?
Others claim him, too.
They hold out hands of promise,
Offering him a fuller life than I can give alone.
Is he mine?
Is he theirs?
Show me, God,
Whose is this child I call "my child."
If he is truly mine,
Make me truly his parent.

3
Is He Lost?

After the pastor had talked with a group of fourth graders, he asked those who were interested in knowing more about what becoming a Christian means to raise their hands. Four children did. Let's take a look at these ten-year-olds who had not at that time made professions of faith.

First, there was Paul, a typical boy, much like Tom Sawyer or Huckleberry Finn. An average student in school, he seldom took on Sunday School activities which involved much reading, though actually he was not lacking in reading skills. Paul quickly raised his hand when the pastor made the request.

Later I talked with Paul's mother. I wanted her to know of the interest Paul had shown. She told me Paul had been asking questions about conversion. He had even told his parents that he had almost responded to the invitation in a recent service which he attended in another church. His interest was deep and genuine.

Next, there was Don, one of the sharpest and most earnest children in the room. Like Paul's parents, Don's parents were regular attenders at Sunday School and worship services and were equally active in other phases of church life. They were not surprised that Don had expressed such an interest, though they had not seen any signs of such interest other than a few, fairly typical comments scattered over a rather long period of time. They and I felt that Don's concern was just beginning. We agreed that his concern should be nourished and encouraged to grow.

John's case was similar and yet distinctive. He had said not one word to his parents about what had taken place in the department. Both of them, however, had noticed that he was unusually quiet on the way home from church that morning. They expressed appreciation for my talking with them. They agreed to keep alert to opportunities that came to them to help John reach a decision. One thing that impressed them greatly about the situation was how differently John had reacted than had his older brother in similar circumstances. That boy, his mother said, talked and talked about his concern. She was 100 percent right when she observed that no two, not even brothers close together in age, can be expected to react in precisely the same way.

The fourth child was Martie. Martie is a slow learner. Her mother revealed to me that Martie had talked earlier about joining the church. That conversation came after a discussion with her playmates, most of whom were already members of the church. Some of these playmates had teased Martie about not being a church member. Martie had expressed her disgust that she could not take the Lord's Supper and asked her mother then why she could not be baptized. Her mother had explained carefully why one is baptized, and Martie had appeared to be satisfied.

As I watched Martie's conduct in the department during the next several weeks, I felt fairly confident that Martie was yet some time away from making a lasting commitment to Christ as her Savior. Her raised hand seemed to indicate more an interest in doing what the others were doing than a sense of personal conviction.

About which child's spiritual condition would you be most

concerned immediately following the pastor's visit? Martie?
Don? John? Paul?

Safe or Saved?

To answer that question about concern for the four children,
one must make some judgments about the inner lives of the
children. Such judgments are extremely difficult to make. Still
most of us would likely feel that Paul needed more direct and
immediate guidance than any of the other three. We might
also be inclined to feel that Martie with her learning problem
lacked the maturity of the others but would, in time, reach
their level of development.

The difference in our thoughts about these two children is
rooted in a feeling, however poorly defined, that a person is
somehow provided for within God's providence until he reaches
the point at which he realizes his true spiritual condition. Then
he must make a decision which determines whether he is to
be saved or lost.

Where does this idea come from? Is there any scriptural
basis for it? The truth of the matter is that the New Testament
tells us very little about children and salvation or even about
children and their relationship to the church. For some reason,
the New Testament writers did not specifically set down the
practices and ideas of the first-century church in relationship
to children.

New Testament teachings do make plain the value which
Christ placed upon children. We are warned against creating
problems for "these little ones" (Matt. 18:7). And we are told
that the angels of the little ones "do always behold the face
of my Father which is in heaven" (Matt. 18:10).

William B. Coble has a significant word to say at this point
in *Children and Conversion*. He points out that Paul's basic
view of the nature of sin may be found in Romans 1:18 to

3:26. Then he summarizes: "There he [Paul] spelled out in detail the fact that sin is the problem of the manner of thinking and acting of the mature person, not the problem of the baby. Paul described the sinner as one who has had ample opportunity to see the reality of God's nature through the world in which he lives." [1]

One wonders about the meaning of the compulsion which many people feel to evoke a profession of faith from children at a very tender age. Does/it somehow show a lack of faith that God is himself more deeply concerned for the children than are these "evangelists"? Can we not trust God to deal with children who have not yet reached accountability? Or must we find ways to get them to nod assent to magic words in order to placate an angry God who might otherwise cast them into hell?

We must not forget that the Bible does not offer one way of salvation for children and another way for adults. The basics in the conversion experience are the same regardless of the age of the person. Accountability is inevitably related to one's ability to deal with the basic truths of the gospel. Until one reaches this point, he is scarcely to be judged accountable.

For a thoughtful discussion of accountability read Chapter 6 of *Children and Conversion*. Dr. William Hendricks summarizes these basics in terms of hearing and affirming certain facts and in terms of having faith in God who brought the facts to be.

"The basic points of the message of the early church are as follows: (1) Jesus came from God, the God of Israel who made heaven and earth. (2) Men killed Christ. The idea is later broadened to assert that all men and man as a unit in his sinfulness is responsible for Christ's death. (3) Yet, Christ's death

---

[1] Clifford Ingle (ed.), *Children and Conversion* (Nashville: Broadman Press, 1970), pp. 57-58.

was according to God's plan. That is, God was acting through Christ's death to bring man to himself. (4) Christ is raised. God in Christ has conquered even man's last enemy, death. (5) God through Christ has sent the Holy Spirit to bear witness to what God in Christ has done for man." [2]

When Dr. Hendricks speaks of faith in God, he is talking about something a lot deeper than a childish affirmation that "I love God" or "God is good." He suggests that the faith which brings salvation "is accompanied by despair of oneself and all other created things. This despair is evidenced by repentance. Repentance involves sorrow for sin. It is sorrow for having trusted in oneself, for having rejected God as alone worthy of our confidence, and for having sought all things for our own gain and desires." [3]

Neither Dr. Hendricks nor any other thoughtful person would, of course, say that a child must express these feelings in adult terms in order to be saved. Still one cannot flippantly dismiss the child's needs to come to these understandings.

A few years ago a study was done with a group composed of Southern Baptist evangelists, pastors, ministers of education, ministers of music, seminary and college professors, counselors, theologians, church children's workers, denominational workers, and parents. The study focused on adult concepts of children's worship, but it included several points related to children and conversion.

Only slightly over 4 percent of the group were willing to say that a church should assume any child lost before age nine. Some were unwilling to say a person is lost before age fifteen to sixteen! And about 30 percent of those responding did not attempt to state an age at which a person should automatically be considered lost.

---

[2] *Ibid.*, p. 91.

[3] *Ibid.*, p. 92.

Eighty-nine percent of the respondents agreed that many children were joining the churches in their denomination without having had a conversion experience. About 85 percent of these felt that children were interpreting some other emotional or inner experience as conversion.

When one considers these responses, he is faced with at least one conclusion: People who are in good position to know and understand children and conversion recognize the pitfalls in attaching accountability to a given age. They also recognize the complexity of the conversion experience. We may need also to grow in our ability to trust God more completely in helping us deal with children, rather than setting norms or standards of our own.

For You to Do

Take a moment now to examine your own conversion experience. Have you tried seriously to think through what was involved in it? Often as we think back on our conversion experience, we become more concerned with where the event took place and with the external circumstances than we are with the transaction which took place within us. Personally when I am asked to relate my conversion experience, I am likely to tell about the old-time Junior department of which I was a member. I will recall the boy who sat beside me as our pastor talked to us. Odom was also nine years old. He had made a profession of faith some months before. When opportunity was given for boys and girls to express their faith in Christ as personal Savior, Odom spoke to me about his own experience. But these details are the externals. The heart of my conversion is what took place between me and God.

Now you should be ready to evaluate these suggested guidelines for dealing with the matter of a child's accountability. To what extent do you agree with each of these statements?

How would you reword the statements to make them more acceptable from your viewpoint?

● Trying to understand accountability is far more important than trying to determine a specific age at which a child may be judged as lost.

● The age at which any one child reaches accountability may vary rather widely from the age at which another child reaches accountability.

● Watering down Bible teachings about conversion so that any child can respond affirmatively to an invitation to accept Christ is a dangerous business.

● Respect for the work of the Holy Spirit in the conversion of the individual requires one to abandon mechanical approaches to helping children become Christians.

● In dealing with a child, one must respect his capacities, neither overrating nor underrating them.

● While one cannot expect a child to express his inner life in adult language or in terms of adult experiences, there is a point beyond which basic truths cannot be simplified and reduced just to make the "evangelist" feel good about a child's apparent decision.

A Parent's Prayer

Dear God,
Help.
Help me understand the inner life of this child of
  mine.
    Help.
Help me respect him as a person.
      Help.
Help me to understand the truths of the gospel.
Help.
Help me to be honestly and deeply concerned about

the possible lostness of my child.
Help.
Help me to settle for nothing less than truth in dealing
with my child.
Help me to wait patiently for the guidance of thy
Spirit.
Help.

4
Would You Believe What He Did?

If you ask a parent whether his child is spiritually precocious, you will likely get a modest answer. But if you listen to a group of parents talking informally—ah! that's another story. Nearly every parent you meet can tell you a score of stories which would, taken at face value, convince you that his child is some sort of spiritual genius.

And no wonder. Children are spiritually perceptive. They do have spiritual sensitivity. They do have experiences which demonstrate their perception and sensitivity.

Take, for instance, two preschoolers in my neighborhood. A woman across the street had died suddenly after an emergency trip to the hospital. Now the mother of one of the preschoolers was about to go to the hospital to have another baby. This preschooler's little neighbor was overheard offering comfort: "Karen, your mother is going to do fine. She will bring you a new baby. Nothing will happen to her."

Take, for instance, the day that five-year-old Donna's beloved dog died. Donna and her mother had a long, heart-to-heart talk as mothers and children must do in such crises. Donna brightened considerably as she expressed conviction that her dog was in heaven.

"Donna, dogs don't go to heaven when they die. Only people go to heaven. This is the way God has planned things."

Once again Donna was in tears. Looking up at her mother, she sobbed, "I wish he was a God dog."

Or take the following conversation between a father and his nine-year-old, who had not at that time made a profession of faith.

"Daddy, Jesus didn't have a real body, did he?"

"Yes, Neal, he really did. But what gave you this idea?"

"Just listening to things in Sunday School and listening to what Dr. _____ says in his sermons," was Neal's response.

"I think you have probably misunderstood some things. The idea you have is an old, old one. But can you remember some times we have read in the Bible about when Jesus got tired or hungry just as we do?" Daddy continued. Then he explained further about Jesus' body, emphasizing that Jesus had suffered genuine pain to save men.

After the explanation, Neal was silent for a moment. Then he spoke again: "Daddy, Jesus was kind of like Abraham Lincoln."

Thoughtfully, Daddy said, "Tell me what you mean."

"Well, Lincoln was so sorry for the slaves that he was ready to do whatever he could to make them free. He wasn't a slave, but he knew how they felt."

You can match these stories with a dozen of your own. And you can add a jillion more told by other parents as evidence that their children are deeply and unusually spiritual. Some of these stories you have listened to with patience, concealing amusement because you didn't think the stories proved anything much—except, maybe, that the parent was typically proud of his child.

Why Parents Misread the Signs

You may even have asked yourself why parents seem so easily deceived by their children's comments. Why are parents so eager to interpret their children's conduct as indicating superior spiritual insight?

The basic reason may be that most of us are predisposed to think of our children as bright. From time to time, we temporarily face the fact that our children are actually fairly typical. Still it is extremely difficult for most parents to be impartial. And love does have its right to cast its aura, too.

Another basic reason we exaggerate the importance of our children's actions is that few of us have good yardsticks by which to measure. We have been children, of course, but that was years ago. Even if we have three, four, five, or six children, their number is very slight compared to the total number of children in the whole country. Even those who work with children at church or in professional life have a *parent* relationship only with the boys and girls in their homes.

A third major reason why we "overinterpret" the evidences of our children's spirituality is rooted in a desire to find genuine evidence of spiritual growth. We can see many evidences of their growth in other areas. They obviously grow taller and heavier. They plainly acquire learning skills such as reading and writing. Their development of social graces is apparent. Almost daily their physical skills, such as bike riding, swimming, and horse riding, open up new avenues for them.

But the picture is not so clear in the area of spiritual growth. You can't back a child up to a wall and measure his spiritual development. No wonder parents are eager to catch any sign of maturing, any reassurance that their efforts to get their children into groups at church and the struggle to answer all those hard questions are paying off.

While we are examining our tendency to overreact to the seemingly spiritual things our children do, let's be honest about another thing. Most of us are competitive. We cannot comfortably sit silent while others tell about their children. We must tell about ours. We try to prove to ourselves and to others that our children are brighter, dumber, faster, slower, more skilled, more clumsy than the children of others. No wonder we grab at signs that they may be more "spiritual" than the average run of children.

Another major reason that we misinterpret the actions of our children is that we tend to take a child's words at adult face value. If our neighbor tells us that he feels God very near to him, we interpret the remark in terms of our own adult experience. We know that he means he is experiencing God's daily sustaining power. When our child says a similar thing, we may interpret his remark in terms of our own adult experience. However, a child might only be telling us that he has the idea that God is hiding behind a nearby tree rather than that the child is feeling the comfort and support of God in a crisis.

Some Seeming Insights

Would it be helpful if we looked at some of the insights which many children have prior to their conversion? The look may prove frustrating if these insights are the very ones which you have taken as evidence of your child's spiritual precocity. Don't be too surprised if we hit one or two like that.

A magazine designed for parents of children under four years of age ran a special feature in each issue composed of stories readers sent in. I wish you could read the submissions, all of them. The most startling thing was the amazing similarity of the submissions. You name something a child did in Dallas which showed unusual sensitivity to God or to others, and your story was matched almost word for word with a story from Duluth. And another striking thing about the submissions was the terrific enthusiasm with which these events were greeted wherever they happened.

"Jesus loves me" is a statement that nearly all children reared in the church make long before they begin to think about becoming Christians. Most parents take this statement for what it really means—and it may mean somewhat different things at different times in the life of the child. However, too many parents and workers, too, see in this simple statement much more than it really means. To these people the statement seems to be a theological pronouncement upon a restored relationship between the sinner and his Maker. These people are willing to accept the statement as proof that a child has realized at the adult level what it means to be loved by one's personal Savior.

"I love Jesus" is another statement children who go regularly to Sunday School learn to make early in life. Some of us, parents and workers, are prone to think that "love" used with "I" and "Jesus" means something vastly different to a young child than when he uses "love" in connection with other words— words like mommy, daddy, Santa Claus, Uncle Bob. The child's saying, "I love Jesus," can make a parent rejoice, but it may not mean that the child has committed his heart and life to Christ. We do well to remember that most church children are virtually programed to make the two statements we have just discussed. In the settings in which such children are reared, a child may learn to make these statements and to repeat them frequently for the rewards he receives, quite apart from feeling any real emotion as he says them.

"God loves everyone" may be said by almost any church-conditioned child old enough to pronounce the syllables. Saying the words does not, however, mean that the child has much of a concept of "everyone." He may mean no more than that God also loves his playmates. Or he may use the statement in connection with thoughts about children around the world. In this case, we need to remember that his concept of the little child in remote Tibet and the child in far away Patagonia is blurred with the same vagueness that hazes the child's mental picture of kids down the street whom he seldom sees. To take the statement at face value is foolish. The younger the child, the more likely it is that the statement is little more than an echo of some teacher or parent. But the child will grow. As he does, this simple statement will become laden with more and more significance for him.

Another idea which many children develop long before they have any sense of personal guilt or sinfulness is that people do bad things but God forgives them. Children develop a sense that some things are right and some things are wrong long before they see any connection between their actions and God.

An eight-year-old talked with her brother about becoming a Christian. Finally she said in utter frustration, "I don't understand."

Her brother, who was several years older, responded gently: "One day you will know that what you do affects God. He really does care what you do. When you know that, then you will understand a lot that bothers you now."

A group of seven-year-olds was looking at present-day pictures to discover who in the pictures was doing something for which he would need forgiveness. The leader had not pressed them to think in terms of God's forgiveness so much as the forgiveness of others. Interestingly enough in one picture they identified the culprit as "the boy in green."

"And what is he doing that he will need to be forgiven for?" the leader asked.

"He is running in the church, and he will wake up the baby."

Only after this response did the adults in the room become aware that among the people in the picture was a young couple with a baby.

You can guess what a good many of these seven-year-olds

had been doing which had brought down parental wrath. In the young child, a sense of right and wrong is usually quite pragmatic. That which displeases mother or daddy or other powerful adult figures is wrong. The same act going undetected and, therefore, invoking no displeasure may not be considered wrong. In time the child outgrows this stage, but for some time he relates wrongness or rightness to the capacity of actions to please or displease parents rather than to the effect of the same actions upon God.

As children begin to understand the idea that God forgives, they may or may not connect this forgiveness with Christ's life, death, and resurrection. We are assuming too much when we let a child's open talk about God's forgiveness tempt us to conclude that the child has developed more than a very immature idea about reconciliation.

Occasionally one encounters an adult who reads too much into another type of statement children make. This type of statement appears to show concern about one's ultimate destiny. When a child says, "I want to go to heaven when I die," what does he mean? Until he has a fairly well-developed concept of death, it is extremely unlikely that he has weighed alternatives and thought through the consequences of actions taken in this life in relationship to eternity. Many a child who makes such a statement wants equally to go to Pasadena or Orlando or wherever he is convinced people go to have a good time.

Perhaps the statement which gives parents the most trouble is "I want to be baptized." Just what does a child mean by these words? If you have a young child in your home who has not yet told you this, be prepared. What he means is, of course, a reflection of his maturity. The older he is, the more likely he is to mean what you are likely to assume he means.

If he is quite young, he may be telling you that he wants to get in on whatever there is to get in on. He may be entranced with the ritual which surrounds the ordinance of baptism. And the more ceremony there is, the more he may be intrigued.

Or he may be telling you that he wants the status which he is aware that others acquire by being baptized. He may be quite sensitive to the approval bestowed upon another child who has been baptized. The action, he figures, must be right; didn't it rate a lot of adult approval?

Remember Martie? Her expressed desire to be baptized was linked primarily to peer approval. She rightfully resented the teasing she received because she could not be a participant in the Lord's Supper in her own church.

Being free to partake of the Lord's Supper is another good translation of "I want to be baptized." Children grow weary of being excluded from what they see as an important ritual in which others in the church engage. They are told that they may take part after they are baptized. So, what would *you* want to do in their circumstances? Be baptized, of course.

For a moment, let's think about another way in which children confuse parents about their spiritual perceptions. This way is a bit broader than the uttering of statements which we have been looking at. This way involves quoting and applying Scripture. When a child can quote a verse and can verbalize an application of it, what parent is not thrilled. Our thrill might, perhaps, be diminished if we watched more closely to observe nonverbalized applications of the same truth.

A toddler just conquering the beginnings of speech learned a familiar Bible verse from his grandfather. You can guess that the verse was, "Be ye kind."

The child did not forget the verse. In fact, he continued to quote it for several years. He heard it at home and at Sunday School. Supposedly he was exposed to practical applications of the verse in a variety of situations. But he continued to apply the verse in a very restricted way for a long time. Until

he was well into his school years, he used the verse like a
club when someone failed to treat *him* as he wished to be
treated. Somehow he just didn't see that the verse meant *he*
should be kind to others.

As is true of adults, the child's ability to quote Scripture
is not exactly the same thing as the ability to understand and
apply Scripture. We may take justifiable pride in our children's
learning favorite verses and great passages from the Bible. We
must, at the same time, observe their conduct with a clear
eye and listen to their conversation with a sensitive ear if we
are accurately to assess their spiritual insights.

For You to Do

Are you currently struggling to understand the true level
of your child's spiritual development as he seems about ready
to make a profession of faith? If so, this next "exercise" is
just for you.

If you do not currently find yourself in this situation, perhaps
you are dealing with a child in your church who is on the
verge of this decision. Yet you are troubled about the situation.
If so, the "exercise" is for you, too.

Here it is: Take time now to list at least three evidences
of the readiness of the child for conversion. Perhaps you wish
to list more than three evidences. Good.

Now evaluate each of these evidences by asking these basic
questions:

• Is this evidence one which is fairly common among children of this age? That is, do playmates and friends often say
or do such a thing without giving any other evidence of having
reached a genuine confrontation with Christ?

• What has the child said when you have asked him to tell
you more about what he means by his words or deeds?

• Does the evidence rest mainly upon a statement in the

"language of Zion" rather than upon words which the child uses in his own individual and original way?

Arriving at honest answers to these questions is not always easy. A lot of subjective judgment is needed. In fact, a lot of sanctified judgment is needed before one reaches a hard-and-fast decision about the conclusion to which the evidence points. Pray as you seek to evaluate the evidences. You can trust God who richly bestows wisdom upon those who ask.

One Word of Caution

If your child is unusually young at the time he appears to be facing the conversion experience, may I make an additional suggestion at this point? Frequently, parents and workers face such times with only one question in mind: Is he really bright enough at this age to understand what he is doing?

Any response to this question is likely to be confused by our own prejudiced appraisals of the child's innate abilities. Our responses are also cluttered by a well-based reluctance to limit the work of the Holy Spirit in the child's life. Maybe the child isn't all this exceptional, we say to ourselves, but who are we to say that the Holy Spirit cannot work this grace in him.

Indeed, who are we to so limit the work of the Holy Spirit? None of us would presume to do so. But we may reasonably ask ourselves another question: Does God wish to deal with my child on an unusual basis?

The scriptural evidence for God's intrusion into the lives of very young children in unusual ways is not abundant. Samuel's call did not come the year that Hannah brought him to the Temple to stay with Eli. Jesus' stay at the Temple came about the time any Jewish boy would be admitted into full adult responsibility in the congregation.

A thoughtful parent has only one answer to this last question:

"So be it." If God is so dealing with your child, you can trust him to provide you the guidance you need to help your child. You need not fear that God will cease to deal with the child forever if you are slow in coming to a full understanding of what is taking place.

A Parent's Prayer

Dear Lord,
Can it be you who calls to my child?
Even Eli did not at first understand whose voice broke the night.
Forgive me if I am slow to understand.
Give me the words to help my child respond to your call.
Sometimes I lack the courage even to leave him where he may hear thy words.
I am no Hannah, no Elkanah.
Yet I would not confuse this child.
Help me give him to thee in thy time and in thy way.
Most of all, help me to help him give himself to thee
            In his way
            In thy time.

5
What Are the Signs?

"I just don't know how to tell whether or not Sue is under conviction," Betty all but moaned to Sue's Sunday School teacher.

Of course, the matter under consideration was a most important one. But Betty had dealt with other important events in Sue's life with considerably less anxiety than she seemed to be experiencing now. Why do you suppose that Betty, like many other parents, was so befuddled by the signals she thought she was picking up from Sue?

At least a part of the reason rests in the fact that most parents are skilled in picking up the signs of a child's feelings in many other areas of his life. For instance, almost as soon as his child is home from the hospital, a parent learns how to tell when the child needs to void his bladder or bowels. Something in the child's expression or a twist of his body betrays the child's condition to his alert parent.

Who needs a thermometer to detect a child's fever? Haven't you long since learned the peculiar quality which fever brings to the nape of the neck or to the forehead of your child? Or maybe your child has some other "detecting" spot.

After the onset of school days, a parent can usually tell when his child has had a difficult day. The child may tell you that all is okay. But the droop of his head or the slope of one shoulder says something different.

Neighborhood scraps are revealed by black eyes, of course. But wouldn't you know by your child's silence that he had been mixing it up with the kid next door? Or sometimes he tips his hand by being overly cheerful.

How often do you ask, "Did you do what I told you to do?" and then wonder why you bothered to ask? Something told you that the answer was no before your question was half completed. Was it a look around your child's eyes? Never mind, you know the sign.

But to get signs which you do not know how to interpret or to think a condition exists and be unable to find any signs— ah, here is a troublesome situation. No wonder parents are bewildered over the signs of conversion.

Signs to Spot

Let's take another look at the four children we talked about in chapter 3: Martie, Don, Paul, and John. What signs of conviction could a parent have discovered in each of these children about the time they raised their hands in the department?

A common sign of a child's growing interest in becoming a Christian is questions. Has your child begun to ask questions about actions and ideas related to becoming a Christian? He may be approaching the time of decision. His questions surely indicate that he is in need of information, whether the information is to be used immediately or later. Any child's questions are shaped by his particular experiences, but here are some questions which children commonly ask:

Why do people get baptized?

What do you say to the preacher if you go down to the front?

Am I a Christian?

Can I give my heart to Jesus?

What are you supposed to do if you are a Christian?

Did Jesus die for my sins?

Do I have sins?

What is sin?

What will happen to me when I die?

Why did Jesus have to die?

Do you think I should join the church?

In many children a sign of being under conviction is a shift in their usual level of activity. Of course, hyperactivity is a relative thing. If your child has always been an exceedingly active child, you may or may not be able to see any change in his behavior. If, on the other hand, your usually quiet child becomes a loud and aggressive person, he may be indicating to you that something deep and troubling is going on inside him.

However, remember John. His mother indicated that he was unusually quiet and thoughtful, although he did not come out and tell what had happened in the department. So we might add quietness as a possible sign of conviction.

Another possible sign of a child's growing conviction about his spiritual condition is exaggerated fears. Like the other signs, this sign is not found in all children. A nine-year-old boy came under conviction one evening as he listened to the preacher. During the several weeks which passed before he faced up to the decision before him, he felt threatened in situations which he had once accepted as normal. If the short distance from his home to the church had to be walked alone at dusk, the shadows seemed peopled with unseen persons or things.

Exaggerated fears may break out in a variety of forms. A child may feel that he cannot do at all what he normally does well. He may be reluctant to try new experiences even though he has always been a daring adventurer.

Some children develop a more lively, even an intense, interest in Bible study. A parent who works closely with his child in preparation for Sunday School and other church experiences will usually notice this interest. A Sunday School teacher certainly may notice a change in the quality of a child's interest. Even though increased interest in the Bible may come from other sources, it is worth noting as a possible sign of conviction.

Don't despair, however, if your child does not evidence an intense interest in the Bible and in his church experiences. Do not dismiss the possibility that he is under conviction. Like many adults, many children want to escape from the experiences which make them uncomfortable. If your child has ever had a siege of "schoolitis," a condition usually occurring on Monday morning and accompanied by pains lasting until a half hour or so after school begins, you can recognize "Sunday Schoolitis." Of course, the child is not likely to tell you the real reason he would like to stay home; he may not understand that much about himself.

Conversation which a child initiates can give clues. When the child takes the lead and moves the conversation to spiritual matters or to matters closely related to the church and its life, he may need further help in thinking seriously about becoming a Christian.

A few words of caution are in order at this point. A child could have all of the symptoms which we have described—even alternating between hyperactivity and intense preoccupation—without actually being ready to consider becoming a Christian. In normal growth many children move through periods of acute interest in the Bible and in matters related to the inner life before they come under conviction.

Any child's "symptoms of spirituality" are distinctively his. While one finds a great deal of similarity from child to child, each child tends to develop his own patterns. This individuality of symptoms often tips off a parent that something special is taking place.

Just for a moment ask yourself how you are able to detect signs in other areas of your child's life. You see a grimace; you hear a silence; you sense an attitude. In nearly all of these instances, the signs are obvious to you because they mark a deviation from the usual.

One of the best ways to prepare to note signs of conviction in your child is to know him well. If possible, begin now to know him, rather than waiting until you begin to suspect that he may be facing life's most important decision. Then deviations in his usual pattern will indicate to you that something significant is taking place in his life. Knowing him well, you will know that this "something significant" is most certainly the conviction which leads to conversion.

For You to Do

Here is a question which you may find helpful as you think about your own child or about another child in whom you are particularly interested:

If your parents (or church-school teachers) had assessed your inner life by your outward actions during the time you were under conviction, what conclusions would they have reached? Do you think they could have told that you were under conviction?

Now, can you list some of the signs they would (or could) have noted?

_____

_____

_____

_____

And what are the signs you see in that child in whom you are especially interested?

_____

_____

_____

_____

Who Makes the Decision?

Having reached the conclusion that your child must be under conviction, how do you confirm your diagnosis? In an obvious way: Talk directly with the child about his feelings. You don't need to say, "Look here, I think you are under conviction; and I can tell you just what to do." But you can indicate that you are wondering what is on his mind. You may safely lead him to talk, though you will certainly avoid forcing him to a decision before he is ready.

As parents, we do make a lot of decisions for our children. When you get right down to it, most of us decide what ours will eat, the hours they will sleep, what they will watch on television, how often they will bathe (and how thoroughly)— even if some of these decisions seem to be made more by default than by design.

But the decision to accept Christ as Savior is one decision which we cannot make for our children. This decision is one which a person makes for himself whether he is a child, a young adult, middle-aged, or in the golden years. A parent may maneuver his child into going through the motions of appearing to profess personal faith in Christ. He may persuade a child to join a church. He may fool himself, even for the rest of his life. Still, if a child becomes a disciple of the Master, the transaction is between him and God. The ability to diagnose another's spiritual condition is not the same thing as the power to make his spiritual decisions for him, not even in the case of a parent and a child.

A Parent's Prayer

Dear God,

I have caught her almost inaudible moan in the long night and have found fever at my fingertips.

I have held her for shots and forced medicine through her clenched lips.

I have made her turn her hands over for inspection,

And I have sent her back to wash again.

I have heard sassiness in her tone;

I have, for her good, insisted on courteous speech.

I have quizzed her and discovered unstudied lessons; then driven her to her books.

Now, Lord, I need sensitivity to know her spiritual needs.

And grace, Lord, I need grace to help her face you Herself.

6
How Do You Talk Religion to a Child?

Are you bilingual?

Or do you speak only English?

If you are an adult Christian, you are likely bilingual, at least in a sense.

You probably speak a special religious vocabulary altogether foreign to children. Sometimes we refer to this kind of talk as the "language of Zion." The language consists of terms which adult Christians have used for generations. These terms have meaning to those who understand them but are often confusing to the uninitiated. A person usually becomes initiated by listening to many sermons and by singing the great old hymns over and over.

This language can be translated into everyday children's English. Sometimes, however, the more conservative among us feel that extreme liberty has been taken with sacred terms. And the task is not easy at best.

One problem which confronts the would-be translator is his own insensitivity to the difficulty of the language. To him the words seem to be ordinary, everyday English with perfectly obvious meanings.

A Child's Glossary of Common Terms

Would you like to try your hand at translating some terms

from the language of Zion into child's language? Suppose you read the terms in the left-hand column without paying attention to the other column. (To play safe, cover the right-hand column.) Once you have read the left-hand column, read the items in the other column. That column suggests what each term might mean to a child. See how closely your ideas agree with mine.

Language of Zion	Child's Translation
Go (come) forward	Move from where one is seated to the front of the auditorium
Commit your life	Who knows? "Commit" is a strange word.
Give your heart	Take my heart out of my body and hand it to someone? Send a valentine?
Take Jesus as Savior	Go somewhere with Jesus.
Lost	Misplaced; gone; maybe taken by someone who wanted it; not knowing where you are
Saved	Kept in a hiding place, like saving pennies or dollars
Make a profession	Build something called a profession?
Give the preacher your hand	Maybe shake hands with the preacher?
Privileges and responsibilities of church membership	Something they give you when you join the church or get baptized
The hand of Christian fellowship	Somebody's hand; maybe the hand of a Christian; maybe there's someone named Christian Fellow Ship— what a name!
Be baptized	Let the preacher put you under the water

Some Common Terms Translated

Now let's try our hand at translating the terms into words which a child can understand. If you find this exercise a bit dull or think it pointless, consider the alternatives to developing such a skill. We can go on talking to children about becoming Christians in terms they do not understand. Maybe we can kid ourselves that trying to communicate with people without talking their language is intelligent. Let's not let ourselves suspect that God is less than pleased with our indifference to the problem.

Or we can tell ourselves that eventually the children will grow up and catch on. In the meantime, we may think their failure to understand religious terms is of little consequence.

Or we can take a third view. We can maintain that just learning to speak the language of Zion is the heart of becoming and being a Christian. A lot of Christians appear satisfied with this view.

You don't really care for any of the alternatives? Good. Then let's proceed. You may want to read the left-hand column and make your own translations before checking mine.

Language of Zion	*Translation*
Go (come) forward	Give your heart to Jesus? No. Better try: Let the church people know what Jesus has done for you.
Commit your life	Promise Jesus that you will always try to please him in all you do.
Give your heart	Trust Jesus to help you live as he wants you to live everyday.
Take Jesus as Savior	See the translation for "Give your heart."
Lost	Not trusting Jesus to save you and to help you day by day.

Saved	Trusting Jesus to forgive you for displeasing him. A person is saved when he is willing to live for Jesus all the rest of his life.
Make a profession	Let other people know that you have promised Jesus to try to live always in the way he wants you to live.
Give the preacher your hand	Tell the preacher about the promise you have made to Jesus.
Privileges and responsibilities of church membership	The right to vote in church meetings, the right to take part in the Lord's Supper, the duty to help do the work of the church.
Hand of Christian fellowship	A welcome from the people who are already Christian, usually done by shaking hands at the close of the service in which a person joins the church
Be baptized	Let the preacher put you under the water to show that you are a follower of Jesus.

How Not to Talk

Of course, you saw the flaw in the game we have been playing. Translating difficult terms is not all there is to talking religion to a child. The translations which we have made may fail to fit perfectly into a particular conversation or setting. As is always true of living speech, they must be altered a bit here and a bit there to serve best their intended purpose.

One important rule, perhaps the most important one, in talking to a child about his religious experiences is: Do not *lead* the child. Leading a child to say what you think he should say is an ever-present temptation for an adult. We do our leading in a variety of ways: inflection, statements which are easily repeated, introducing ideas the child is not ready for. But the single way in which we most often lead children is by questions.

Consider for a moment some of the questions which we commonly ask a child when he does "come forward" to "give the preacher his hand":

Are you coming to accept Jesus?

Do you know that you have sinned?

Are you sorry for your sins?

Do you want Jesus to forgive you for your sins?

Do you love Jesus with all your heart?

Do you want to accept Jesus as your Savior?

Are you ready to follow Jesus in baptism?

Do you want to become a Christian?

Do you trust Jesus as your Savior?

Suppose that a child with no background whatsoever did "come forward." Would he know what answer was expected from him in response to any one of these questions or to others like them? Of course, he would.

If this sort of interview is all that a child is given when he indicates interest in becoming a Christian, he has been treated less than fairly. His ability to nod yes at the right time is scarcely evidence of unusual depth of conviction.

Poor questions are not the only way in which children can easily be led. We sometimes lead them with sweeping assertions about how a convert acts or feels. We say to a child: "Everyone has sinned. Everyone must feel guilty for what he has done." Since we have just told him that he is now a believer, he identifies whatever feeling he has as the feeling we have described. Few children are brave enough to disagree flatly with a firm-minded adult, especially an adult for whom the child feels great respect.

Another mistake we make with children is to jump deeper into a subject than they are ready at the moment to go. A good illustration is the story about the child who asked his mother where he came from. After listening patiently to her discourse on how babies are born, he shrugged and commented, "I just wondered. My new friend is from Chicago."

What happens when an adult makes one of these leaps beyond the child? Sometimes the child bluntly stops the adult, and a promising conversation dies. Sometimes the child becomes obviously confused, and the adult realizes his mistake. If neither of these things happens, the adult may remain ignorant of what he has done while the child politely accepts the leading he is given. When the conversation is over, the adult is confident that great good has been accomplished; the child may be more confused than ever.

A child's opening statement in a conversation about religious experience should not immediately be pressed to its limit. As a rule, an adult should ask a few questions of his own to be sure of just what the conversation is going to be about. "Tell me more." "What do you mean?" "Why do you say that?" Such statements and questions give the adult a chance to breathe as he discovers the meaning of the child's comment and checks the level at which the child is prepared to discuss his experiences.

How to Talk

Anyone can talk about how not to do something. The real trick is how to do a thing. Consider these tips for talking religion to a child.

Encourage the child to express ideas in his own words.—You may rest assured that a churchgoing child learns early in life to handle the language of Zion. That is, he learns to use its terms correctly even though he does not grasp their significance.

Unless you encourage a child to express his religious ideas in his own words, you may remain blind to his ignorance.

Two first graders told their public-school teacher that they were to be baptized the following Sunday. The teacher, interested in knowing more about the girls' religious experiences, asked, "What do you mean?"

The girls patiently explained the process of being put under the water by the pastor.

"Yes, but tell me why a person is baptized?" responded the teacher. "What happens to a person after he is baptized?"

The girls' responses dealt altogether with things such as going to Sunday School regularly and with "being good."

One wonders if anyone in the girls' church had helped them put their ideas and feelings into their own words. One prays that their understanding of what becoming a Christian and a church member means ran more deeply than their remarks indicated.

Refrain from offering rewards.—No one gives children pennies for making professions of faith. Yet most of us have at one time or another in one way or another rewarded a child for telling us what we wanted to hear. Adults have a heavy arsenal of rewards at their disposal. Most children do want adult approval, and we express approval in a wide variety of ways.

Take, for instance, the affirmative nod. A child is telling us something. As we listen, we nod affirmatively every time he says something of which we approve. If he wanders from this path, we do not nod. With the speed of a computer he corrects his course.

Take, for instance, expressions such as "That's right" or "That's good." We unconsciously encourage a child by spicing our conversations with such terms.

Or, if you prefer a more extreme example, take out-and-out

expressions of approval: "I'm so happy for you"; "I'm so glad you are thinking about becoming a Christian"; "I'm sure you are going right on with what we have been talking about and will make a profession of faith next Sunday." Such remarks may, of course, be appropriate *after* the child has clearly defined his feelings and intentions. They jump the gun if the child's ideas are only vaguely formed.

Give the conversation a proper value.—When an adult acts as if religious conversation were totally set apart from everyday life, how is a child to feel simple and direct in his approach to religion? How is he to feel that it is normal and natural to think and to talk about God, Jesus, the church, and oneself?

Spiritual matters are not on a par with math problems or the neighbor's cat's kittens. We need not try to keep our tone from hinting that we view spiritual matters in a serious light. However, using one's ordinary, conversational tone says: "Talking over spiritual matters is normal for the two of us. Spiritual concerns are part of our day-to-day living."

Try to be natural and at ease.—Any adult who has taught young children for an extended time has been impressed with how frequently they ask questions which are exceedingly difficult to answer. Somehow their simple remarks veer abruptly into deep theological waters. Nothing amuses an experienced children's worker more than to hear someone remark that he intends to work with children because he won't have to know much about the Bible.

Because children can ask difficult questions with such ease and with such frequency, some of us become nervous about conversations with them. Because children are painfully honest, we are not always at ease in talking with them on any subject. Perhaps because religious matters were not much discussed with us in our own childhoods, we tend to feel uncomfortable in talking religion with children. Nevertheless, being at ease in talking with children on religious topics is extremely important.

Be quiet.—If one is uncomfortable, he frequently talks too much. If one is a bit short on understanding, he usually finds it easier to dominate a conversation than to let the other fellow take the lead. If one is overly eager to make a point, he is likely to take over. If one is nervous, silence makes him more so.

In talking about religious matters and religious experiences with a child, one must adjust to long silences. Waiting patiently while a child tries to shape his own thoughts is one of the best ways to assure him of your interest in and respect for him and his ideas. Sometimes a single word inserted in a silence is fruitful. Sometimes a simple question or comment is productive. But too frequently our adult interjections serve only to throw the child off track.

Accept the child and his ideas.—We nearly always want to gain the full assent of the people with whom we talk. We feel we have failed completely if we do not persuade the other fellow to endorse our view—whether the topic be brands of toothpaste, politics, art, personal relationships, or religion. Letting the other fellow grow to our point of view is difficult. Yet leaving room for such growth is absolutely imperative in the case of children. They seldom disagree with us from sheer perversity or from a desire to dissuade us of our ideas; they do often lack maturity sufficient to enable them to embrace our views. If our views are right, we can trust the child to reach them as he outgrows his immaturity. But we must keep the lines of communication open.

For You to Do

Evaluate the following summary of the thoughts in this chapter. Add to it any other principles which you feel are important.

You can talk religion effectively with your child or the children you teach. Remember these simple principles:

- Don't depend on the language of Zion.
- Avoid the common pitfalls which trap understanding.
- Cultivate good conversational skills.

- Practice your conversational skills with children at every opportunity. Skills developed in talking about all sorts of subjects can stand you in good stead when you want to talk religion.

- Evaluate honestly each conversation you have with a child on any subject to determine your effectiveness in hearing and expressing ideas.

A Parent's Prayer

I suppose, God, that I have all the words I need
To talk with my child about his spiritual life.
What I need is help to know how to put these words
  together.
What I need is awareness of what his words mean to
  him and what he intends them to mean to me.
What I need is sensitivity to what my words mean to
  him.
Perhaps more than I realize, I need grace to:
        accept him as he is;
        let him be a person in his own right;
        live with him as a person, not simply as my
        child.
Dear Lord, give me skill in the language of your love.

7
Where Are the Roots?

For all the years that our children were small, my wife and I listened to the prophets of doom. Parent after parent warned us that the problems we then faced were as nothing compared to what we could expect in the teen years. We thought we could see the generation gap coming. We almost wanted, against our better judgment, to keep our children babies. We could "manage" them.

One day we visited in the home of a friend in another city. "These teen years have been the richest years of all," Arlene told us enthusiastically. "Don't let anyone scare you about them. We feel closer to our three children now than we did when they were small."

Good parent-child relationships in the teen years have roots in earlier years. And the kind of relationship which enables parents to do the best—and easiest—job of helping their children in spiritual matters does not just happen after the children become accountable. Deep roots go back at least to the time of a child's birth.

Maybe your family does not have these roots. You can't pretend roots are there if they are not. But it is never too late to start working toward the qualities which make good roots.

Basic Attitudes

One root involves basic attitudes. You may prefer to think of each of these attitudes as a single root, but they are closely related.

The first root is basic honesty with yourself. No one is as effective as he could be in helping another person if he kids himself about his own spiritual life. A person knows whether he attends worship services with regularity. He knows whether he reads his Bible daily. A person has a fair idea of the total amount of time he spends daily in meditation. Any of us could list the kind deeds he has performed for others in Christ's name in the past month or so. Yet the sum total of all these facts is not equivalent to one's basic attitudes, one's feelings about the place of God in his life. A person can go through the motions of being religious without feeling much of anything. In fact, going through the motions may be easier than taking stock of self.

You need not expect to guide your child into a valid religious experience if you "play games" with your own religious experience. This is not to say that a parent must be morally perfect before he can point his child toward what is right. It does mean that you can't *pretend* perfection and dedication where they do not exist and expect to be an effective guide. The more self-deceived you are about your own experience, the more likely you are to fail in shaping your son or daughter into the image you think is yours.

Linked to honesty with self is honesty in the expression of feelings. We recognize that a child should be encouraged to express his feelings and ideas in his own words. Yet we, as adults, find doing so rather difficult.

As an exercise, try expressing your feeling about some aspect of your religious life. For instance, what does prayer mean to you? How do you feel about praying?

No, not that! Resist the temptation to use common phrases. "Sweet Hour of Prayer" may express your feelings rather well; actually it expressed most clearly the feelings of W. W. Walford. No fair simply picking up his words.

No, again! Try to say what you *do* feel, not what you think you ought to feel. All of us have listened to the testimonies of persons who are powerful in prayer. We would like to be what they are, feel as they do, act as they act. In time, perhaps we shall. For the present, however, we must deal with ourselves where we are. To do so, we must be honest about where we are.

Honesty in expressing feelings is especially important in dealing with children. Out of their limited ability to cope with verbalizations, most children develop extreme sensitivity to tone, inflection, body posture—all the nonverbal clues by which we express feelings. We seldom fool them with words. However dimly they are aware of our dishonesty, they come to distrust us when they sense differences between what we feel and what we say we feel.

Respect for a child as a person is another attitude essential in developing the atmosphere in which a parent can be genuinely helpful in spiritual matters. One is a parent for as long as both he and his child live, even though the parent lives to be one hundred and ten and the child reaches ninety. Nevertheless, the parent-child relationship has unique qualities at different stages in the child's development. Few parents attempt to relate to their grown children in the same ways they related to these children as babies. "Cutting the apron string" goes on across the years; a wise parent recognizes and accepts the responsibility. A father of three children remarked about the shifting of his relationship with his own mother. He said, "For the first time, we were just two adults enjoying each other's company."

Respect for the personhood of other persons is basic in all good human relationships. This quality cannot be ignored between parent and child. Such respect enables a parent to let a child grow in accord with his own personality. One can't, of course, just let a child grow like a cabbage in the patch. Neither can a parent impose his own hopes upon his child.

"Mother always told me that it was a pity I was so plain," said one woman who in middle years had come to terms with her own potential. Actually she was an attractive person, though her attractiveness was rooted more in her spirit than in her physical appearance. Her mother, however, had seen herself as the mother of the belle of the ball. She could not, or would not, settle for anything else. Needless to say she created many problems and heartaches for her child.

Perhaps to some degree every parent is guilty of this sort of thing. Else why are so many children forced through music lessons by parents who never had a chance at such lessons? Else why are parents so quick to accept chances for their children to appear in plays, give speeches, go to parties, play athletic games?

Fortunately most of us stop short of deep and permanent harm to our children. Our love for them overcomes our desire to shape them according to our dreams. We do respect them as persons and recognize their right to be themselves.

Religious Conversation Is Natural

One reason parents have difficulty in talking to their children about conversion is that they have not made apparent to their children the fact that daily life has a religious dimension. Such parents convey to a child the concept that religion is confined to the edges or to a special area of life, rather than permeating all of life.

Let us suppose that you are afraid you might be so failing

your child. Have hope. Assuming that your faith is vital to you, there are steps which you can take to help your child feel that vitality. These steps will make religious conversation a normal, natural part of your life.

The first step is to make prayer a significant element in your personal life. Develop your capacity for communion with the Lord. Do more than present God with a daily list of wants or even needs. Be a listener as well as a talker.

Step number two: Pray frequently with your family. You likely already have prayer at meals. Try expanding this practice to make it mean more to each member of the family. Some conversation about the good things which God has provided for the family could from time to time precede prayer at meals. And who says that prayer at meals can be only a thank-you for blessings received? Pre-meal conversation can also include discussion of needs within the family, among friends, in the community, and in the wide world. Beware, however, lest long, long conversation create antagonism in hungry tummies.

Make prayer a part of family living at other times, too. For instance, include children in the praying you do in times of crisis, such as illness and death. Parents have some concerns which they cannot share with their children. Nevertheless, even a young child needs to become aware that his parents do talk with God about problems.

Of course, family prayer or prayer in the presence of one's children should not be confined to crises and formal or regularly scheduled times. Prayer should sometimes be a spontaneous expression of emotion. Have you not thrilled to great natural beauty and silently thanked God for his acts of creation? Why not say a thank-you like that aloud?

Letting a child see how firmly one's religious faith is woven into the fabric of his daily life requires more than praying and Bible reading. A parent must deliberately introduce into conversation the religious implications of everyday experiences. You encounter a person in need and stop to help him. Why? Likely your good deeds are based in your religious convictions about the worth of individuals and your responsibility to others. You can interpret the experience to your child. The particular words you use will, of course, depend upon his level of maturity. You may say no more than, "I'm thankful to God when I can help someone."

Maybe other people conveniently ignore a traffic law. You choose to obey it. Your child is aware of what you have done. You can help him understand your obedience to such laws is necessary to you in order to meet your responsibility to God in civil life. Of course, you may first have to overcome the temptation to fuss and complain about those other drivers!

I almost hesitate to make the next statement because it is so easily misinterpreted. Here it is: Let the child sense the importance of your religious faith through involvement, yours and his, in the life of your church.

Many Christian parents are bewildered when their children do not turn out to be saintly. Over and over again one hears the wail: "But I don't know what we did wrong. We had him in Sunday School every Sunday." Friends of the family say: "His family is so active. Sunday School teachers and all that, you know. How could he have gone so wrong?"

True involvement in the life of a church goes deeper than regular attendance. Involvement of the sort which convinces a child of the validity of one's faith is more than holding positions or even capably performing work in the church's organizations. Involvement means caring deeply what happens in the life of one's church and, therefore, finding a place of service in and through it. Such involvement deepens and broadens one's own spiritual experience. Such involvement focuses family activities and family conversation on things pertaining to the inner life. Such involvement, therefore, opens the way to what we are calling religious conversation.

For You to Do

Take time to assess your situation. The judgment you are about to make is, of course, subjective. The analysis is for you and, perhaps, for other members of your family. Your "score" is neither an achievement nor a failure to be revealed to others. Answer these questions to the best of your ability.

> Is prayer together a part of our family pattern at mealtime?
>> in some form of family worship?
>> in moments of crisis?
>> in moments of rejoicing?
>
> How strong is my own devotional life?
>
> What actions have I taken this week, such as helpfulness to others, which were rooted in my basic Christian convictions?
>
> In how many of these instances did I do or say anything which might help my child realize the religious dimension of my acts?
>
> How frequently this week have I talked with my child about God, Jesus, our church, or the Bible?
>
> Has the general tone of these conversations confirmed my love for and devotion to God, Jesus, our church?
>
> Have I talked with my children this week about the church-related experiences which they have had in recent days?

Never Too Late

Just because you feel that you do not measure up, don't give up. If you listen to the pessimists of the world, you would quit trying to help your child about the time he could toddle. You would be convinced that you had already damaged him irreparably. Early experiences are dramatically important. But remember, the Holy Spirit has been promised to you. Good things beyond the imagination of men wait for those who faithfully seek God's will.

A Parent's Prayer

Teach me, O Father,
To begin now to rest myself and my child in thee.
Teach me to waste no time in regret that time has
already been lost.
Teach me to trust thee to use the moments, days, and
years which are left.
Teach me true respect for myself
And for my child.
Teach me to reveal respect in day-to-day living.
Teach me to see thy hand in my life;
Teach me to show thy hand to others.

8
Who Can Help?

This little book isn't going to answer all your questions. In fact, you probably have some questions right now which aren't answered. If you don't, you will as you help a child with his or her particular spiritual growth problem.

So where else do you go for help? This chapter is intended to call your attention to some possible sources of help. Depending upon your circumstances, some of these sources will be of greater help than others.

Pastor and Parent

The first source I want to suggest is your pastor. And the first area in which you will find his assistance invaluable is your own religious experiences. Many of us have trouble helping children because we have thought only vaguely about our own spiritual life. We refuse to face the questions which pop into our minds. We are content to describe our experiences in the words of others. We let these others interpret our experiences for us. Talking with your pastor about your understandings of your inner life and your adventures in Christian living can prove a great blessing to you—and to him.

Help from Others

Persons other than your pastor can help you in a similar

way. If you belong to an adult Sunday School department, your Sunday School teacher may be able to help you. Some mature Christian whose life you have long admired may also help, or there may be a younger Christian whose depth of experience has impressed you. The person who can help you examine your spiritual life might be living in the same house with you: husband, wife, mother, father, grandparent.

Help of Another Sort

Another area in which you may need help is in understanding your child. Playing psychologist can drive one to a psychiatrist. But being able to guide a child's religious development involves understanding him as a person. And such understanding requires understanding what children of his age are generally like.

One person who can help you is a church staff member who has special responsibility for children: a director of children's work or a preschool director. Or the person might be the minister of education or director of Christian education. Usually a person whose age-group responsibility is narrow can provide more help because he (or she) is a specialist.

Another possible source of help are the persons who staff the church organizations to which your child belongs: his Sunday School teachers, those who guide him in music activities, those with responsibility for him in missions groups, and those who lead him in training organizations. Many of these people have studied carefully the age group with which they work.

I suggest that you talk with such persons in a framework like this: "I have observed this (or that) in my child's behavior. My experience with children is limited, and I am not sure whether this conduct is typical. Can you help me?" This start should open the way to increase your general understanding without putting your helper on the spot to give you an instant and perfect solution to a crisis of the moment.

Beyond Your Church

Other parents are a source of help which should not be overlooked. The main problem with help from this source is that parents frequently assume that any approach which has worked with their children has universal value. Parents sometimes attribute success with their children to their own superior skills and intelligence when actually they have merely "lucked in." With a bit of care, however, you should be able to interpret what others are saying to you for what it is really worth. Talking with a variety of parents who live in a variety of situations also helps you round off the edges of philosophies of child-rearing created out of particular settings.

Outside your church are other sources of help in learning what children are generally like. You may belong to PTA. You may be a member of a child study group, formal or informal. We cannot expect such groups to operate always within a Christian framework because the major concerns of such groups are not precisely the same as those of the church. Still we can learn a lot from such groups. When a doctor talks about the physical characteristics of the elementary-age child, he is talking about our children although he speaks in a secular setting. When a psychologist talks about emotional needs, he can stimulate our thinking and help us deepen insights even though he may not deal specifically with religious needs. Of course, we do well to interpret our findings from such settings in the light of our Christian faith and convictions.

Reading Helps

If you like to read, many books and articles can help you better understand your child. You don't have to take everything you read as if it were divinely inspired. Read and test what you read against your own experience.

To give you a start on reading, let me share some books which we at our house have found helpful. This listing is not intended to be exhaustive. It is simply the kind of thing which one friend shares with another.

Understanding Children, Marjorie Stith. A good starting point if you aren't already an accomplished student of childhood. Well-qualified Dr. Stith talks with us about what makes children what they are. The focus is on children in grades one through six.

Understanding Preschoolers, Anne Gilliland. Basic for parents of children under six. This book enables a parent with even a relatively limited experience in child study to gain basic insights.

How to Parent, Fitzhugh Dodson. On the must list for parents of younger children. Dr. Dodson talks a lot to mothers, but what he says is equally helpful to fathers. You'll like his commonsense, nontechnical approach.

Children's Sunday School Work, Eugene Chamberlain and Robert Fulbright. Chapter 1 discusses briefly the child and Christian conversion. See pages 24-27. The rest of the book is for Sunday School workers.

Children and Conversion, edited by Clifford Ingle. Stiffer reading than the other books mentioned so far. However, this book is well worth the time it takes to read it. If possible, read one whole chapter at a time but never more than that. Allow time between chapters for what you read to soak in. I also found that writing my reactions in the margins helped me understand the authors.

The Struggle of the Soul, Lewis Joseph Sherrill. Unlike most of the other books on our list, this one follows the religious development of the individual throughout the whole life-span. The book can do more than give you tips on handling your child's religious development; it can enrich your own spiritual life. Prepare to dig—and sometimes, perhaps, to disagree.

On Becoming Children of God, Wayne E. Oates. Written for those who teach children and youth, this book traces religious experience from birth through later adolescence. It is not always easy reading, but it is always stimulating.

Help! I'm a Parent, Bruce Narramore. This new book is one we wish we had had earlier. It combines insights from contemporary psychology and basic Bible truths to give parents some practical and specific help. The author's style makes for easy reading, too.

The Resource

Several parents slid into a discussion of how to help a child at the time he expresses serious interest in becoming a Christian. After a few minutes one of them suggested that a lot of the problems parents face is created in parents themselves. He said: "We are really afraid to leave it to God. We seem to feel that if we don't settle the whole matter ourselves, it won't be settled at all."

Let none of us fall into the trap of thinking our child's salvation is dependent solely upon our skills in dealing with him. God loves the child even more than we do. We can trust God to help us help the children whom we love.

A Parent's Prayer

With gratitude, dear God,
I salute all who have helped me on my way.
Open my eyes now to the helping hands extended to
    me.
May I reach out in confidence and appreciation.
Let me accept help happily,
Not for myself alone,
But that I in turn might help others:

My child, first,
Other parents,
Other children,
My church.
As I help these others,
I shall serve thee.

When, Indeed?

Now that you have worked your way through the book, I am sure you think it is high time for me to come right out and answer the question raised by the book title. Reminding you that we have agreed that no one can answer the question without respect for the work of the Holy Spirit, here is my statement.

A child can really believe when . . .

> . . . the Holy Spirit moves in his heart and mind just as the Holy Spirit moves in the heart and mind of all whom he brings to repentance and faith.

> . . . his motives for professing faith in Christ are free from external pressures such as the desires of his parents or the adventures of his friends.

> . . . he is able to relate his own actions to God.

> . . . he can for himself accept the basic truths of the gospel.

> . . . his attitude toward the claims of Christ peaks in a genuine desire to live in a way to please God from this day forward.